Contents

...ary of
...y words
...ext.

3

Meet the Egyptians

More than **5000 YEARS** ago, people we call the ancient Egyptians lived along the banks of the River Nile, in Egypt. The ancient Egyptians built a rich and powerful kingdom which lasted for thousands of years.

MAP OF EGYPT AND THE RIVER NILE

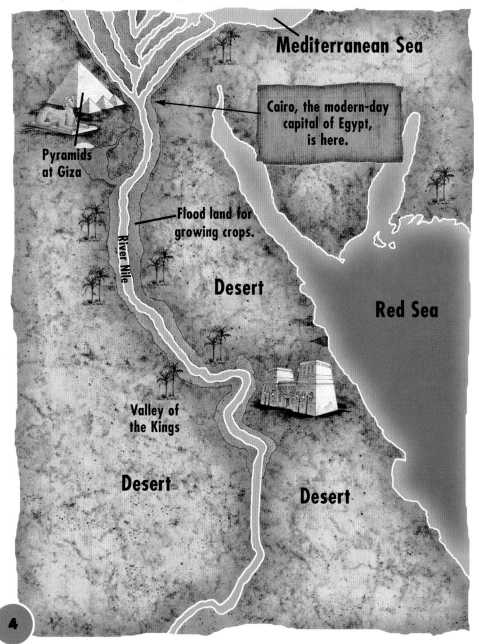

Mediterranean Sea

Cairo, the modern-day capital of Egypt, is here.

Pyramids at Giza

Flood land for growing crops.

River Nile

Desert

Red Sea

Valley of the Kings

Desert

Desert

It is very hot and dry in Egypt. On either side of the River Nile there is sandy, rocky desert.

Every year, the Nile flooded. This made lots of rich, muddy soil which was perfect for growing **crops** in.

The ancient Egyptians used the Nile for travelling around. They sailed boats up and down the river, carrying people and goods.

A model boat from ancient Egyptian times.

At first, boats were made from bunches of reeds. Later, wood was used instead.

Egyptian artefacts

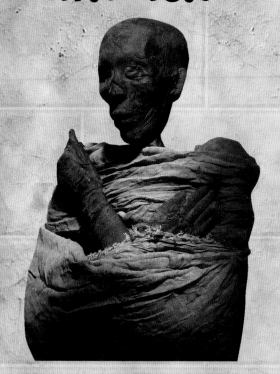

We know a lot about the ancient Egyptians because of the things they left behind, such as their writing, their paintings and MUMMIES!

The ancient Egyptians used pictures, called **hieroglyphs** to write things down.

Amazing mummies

A mummy is a **DEAD BODY** that has been wrapped in bandages. The Egyptians were brilliant at making mummies, and many still survive today. You might be able to see one in a museum.

The ancient Egyptians believed that dead people went to live in another world. For this, they still needed their bodies. So dead bodies were turned into mummies to stop them rotting away.

A mummy mask

Some mummies were put in beautiful **coffins**, decorated with gold and precious stones. Often, a golden mask was put over the mummy's head.

6

Sometimes, the coffin was placed inside a stone chest called a sarcophagus.

Coffin

Mummy

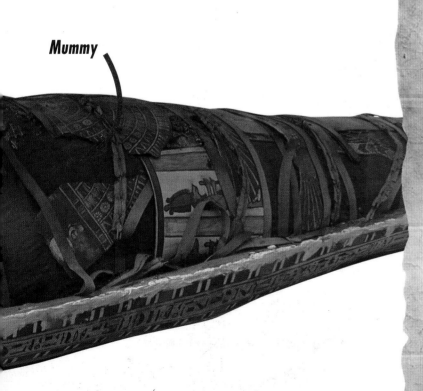

The ancient Egyptians also made animal mummies. This is a mummy of a **PET CAT**.

CROCODILES lived in the River Nile. They were linked to the god of water.

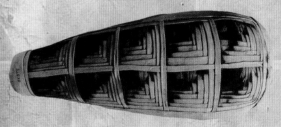

This is an ibis bird mummy. Ibis are water birds. They were **sacred** to the ancient Egyptians.

Making a mummy

The men in charge of **MUMMY-MAKING** were called **embalmers.** The chief embalmer wore a **jackal** mask, because the jackal was the special animal of embalmers.

Anubis, god of embalmers, is shown with a jackal's head.

To make a mummy, you first had to wash the dead body. Next you took the body's insides out and put them in four special jars. Then the brain was pulled out through the nose!

Piles of salt were packed around the body to dry it out. Then you stuffed the body with sawdust or rags and sweet-smelling herbs.

This is the golden coffin of an Egyptian pharaoh (king) called Tutankhamun.

Finally, you rubbed the body with oil and wrapped it in bandages. Then you placed the body in a **coffin**.

Egyptian artefacts

GOOD LUCK charms like this heart **scarab** were tucked in between the bandages.

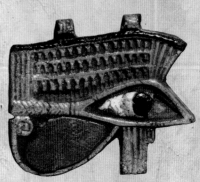

This **MAGIC EYE** charm was thought to protect the mummy in the **Next World**.

These four containers are **CANOPIC JARS**. They held the dead body's lungs, liver, stomach and intestines!

9

Gods and temples

The ancient Egyptians worshipped HUNDREDS of gods and goddesses. They believed their gods made the world and looked after it. In ancient pictures, many of the gods are shown with animal heads!

An ancient temple in Egypt.

The ancient Egyptians built huge **temples** as homes for their gods.

The temples were very important places. Only **priests** could go inside – ordinary people had to stay outside.

An ancient Egyptian painting of a priest.

A statue of the god stood inside the temple. A priest fed and dressed the statue, because the ancient Egyptians believed the god's spirit lived inside the statue.

Priests also said prayers, sang hymns and made **offerings**.

Egyptian gods

This is a model of Ra. He created the world and was the GOD OF THE SUN.

Osiris was the GOD OF THE DEAD. He married Isis, the goddess of women.

Horus was the SKY GOD. He is shown with a **falcon**'s head.

The pharaoh

The **KING OF EGYPT** was also known as the **pharaoh**. He was the most powerful person in the whole country, in charge of all the land and all the people.

The pharaoh lived in great luxury in a palace. He sat on a throne in the Great Hall to carry out his royal duties.

The pharaoh made all the laws and was head of the Egyptian army.

The ancient Egyptians thought the pharaoh was a living god. People came from all over Egypt to ask him to solve their problems and settle their quarrels.

On special occasions, the pharaoh wore a royal crown and a false beard. This ancient statue shows a pharaoh with a beard and crown.

Famous pharaohs

QUEEN HATSHEPSUT was a woman pharaoh, but she still had to wear the royal beard!

TUTANKHAMUN was only nine years old when he became pharaoh.

RAMESSES THE GREAT was a brave soldier. He built lots of **temples** and statues.

Pyramids and tombs

When the first Egyptian **pharaohs** died, their mummified bodies were placed inside **PYRAMIDS** – giant tombs with slanting sides. Some pyramids are still standing.

The biggest pyramid of all is the Great Pyramid at Giza. It took thousands of workers more than 20 years to build.

The pharaohs were buried with magnificent treasures to take into the **Next World**. However, **tomb-robbers** broke into many of the pyramids and stole the treasures!

Over 2.3 million huge blocks of stone were used to build the Great Pyramid.

Some mummies and their treasures were hidden in **tombs**, cut deep into rocky cliffs. But even this was not safe. Many tombs were discovered and robbed.

An uncovered tomb entrance in the Valley of the Kings.

Tutankhamun's tomb

Archaeologists found thousands of TREASURES, like this **pendant**, in Pharaoh Tutankhamun's tomb.

This beautiful BRACELET is decorated with **scarab** beetles.

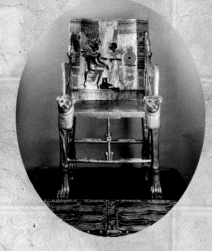

Tutankhamun's GOLDEN THRONE is covered with precious stones.

Egyptians at home

Ancient Egyptian houses were made from dried mud bricks. Rich Egyptians had large houses with gardens. Poor families lived in smaller homes with **JUST ONE ROOM.**

This is a clay model of a poor Egyptian's house.

On hot nights, people slept outside on the roof to keep cool.

The one room was the family's living room, dining room and bedroom!

This model house was found in an ancient Egyptian tomb.

Egyptian food

The ancient Egyptians ate meat, fish, vegetables and fruit. They also ate a lot of tough, gritty bread, which was made from wheat and barley.

Ancient food has actually been found in tombs!

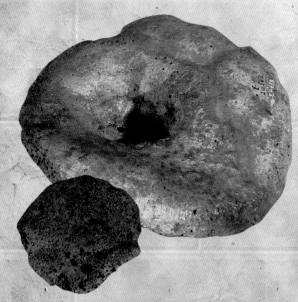

These loaves of Egyptian bread are **3500 YEARS OLD.**

An ancient Egyptian painting showing bread and beer-making.

The ancient Egyptians drank beer made from mashed-up bread. Sometimes it was drunk through a straw to strain out the lumps.

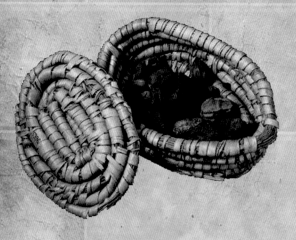

These dates are over **3000 YEARS OLD.** People ate dates fresh or dried.

Egyptian fashion

Ancient Egyptian clothes were light and loose-fitting to keep people cool in the **HOT WEATHER**. Clothes were made from a cloth called **linen**, which was made from plants.

Men wore short, simple **kilts** made from a piece of linen, wrapped around the waist and tied with a knot. A cloak might be worn on top.

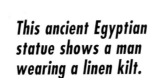

This ancient Egyptian statue shows a man wearing a linen kilt.

18

Women wore long, linen dresses, with linen shawls on top. Sometimes the material was folded into pleats and decorated with colourful beads.

A woman wearing a pleated linen dress.

Ancient Egyptian beads

Both men and women loved to wear make-up and jewellery, such as necklaces, rings and bracelets.

This necklace is made from thousands of tiny beads.

Egyptian artefacts

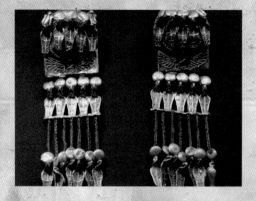

Earrings like these were made from gold and semi-precious stones.

Most people went barefoot, but sometimes they wore sandals made from reeds which grew by the river.

The ancient Egyptians styled their hair or wore wigs.

19

School days

Many ancient Egyptian children did not **GO TO SCHOOL**. Girls helped their mothers at home, while boys went to work with their fathers. Some boys from rich families went to schools run by the **priests**.

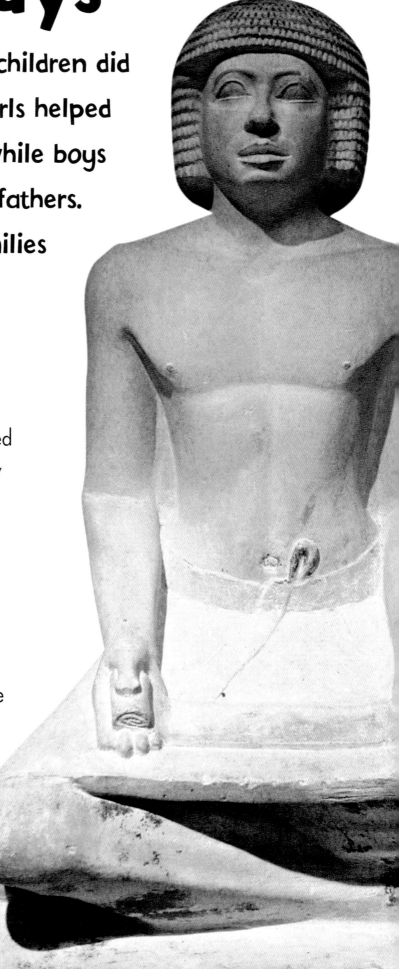

At school, the boys sat cross-legged on the ground. Teachers were very strict, and a lazy pupil might be punished with a beating!

Instead of letters of the alphabet, Egyptian writing used pictures called **hieroglyphs**. Each picture stood for a word or sound. Boys learned to read by chanting long lists of hieroglyphs out loud.

Ancient Egyptian hieroglyphs

Some boys trained to become writers called **scribes**. It took many years, but you could get a good job keeping records for the **pharaoh** or **government**!

An Egyptian scribe

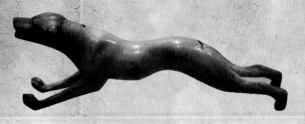

Writing was practised on pieces of wood or broken stone and clay.

Egyptian children had lots of toys, like this ivory dog with a moving mouth.

Off to work

Most ancient Egyptians worked as **FARMERS OR BUILDERS**. Some people worked for the **government** or trained to be **priests** or **scribes**.

This ancient Egyptian painting shows bricks being made.

When the Nile flooded, farmers could not work in their fields, so they took turns to work for the **pharaoh**, building new **temples**, pyramids and **tombs**.

An ancient Egyptian model of a farmer ploughing.

Each November, when the flood had gone down, the farmers ploughed their fields and sowed seed. In March or April, they harvested the **crops**.

The farmers dug small ditches around their fields. They filled these with water from the Nile. They used **shadufs** to pull up water from the river. Some people still use shadufs today.

You can see a shaduf being used in this picture.

Egyptian artefacts

Artists and craftsmen made jewellery, pots and baskets.

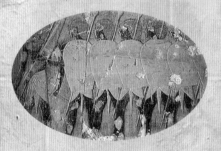

Some ancient Egyptians learned to fight and became soldiers in the army.

Some women worked as dancers. They danced at festivals and parties.

Glossary

ARCHAEOLOGISTS People who dig things up to study history.

ARTEFACTS Items made by people, for example a tool or a pot.

COFFINS Cases in which dead bodies are placed.

CROPS Plants that are grown for food.

EMBALMERS People who made mummies.

FALCON A hunting bird.

GOVERNMENT The people who run a country.

HIEROGLYPHS Ancient Egyptian picture writing.

IVORY A substance that comes from elephant tusks.

JACKAL A wild dog-like animal.

KILTS Short skirts.

LINEN Cloth made from the flax plant.

NEXT WORLD The place where the ancient Egyptians believed your spirit went after you died.

OFFERINGS Gifts from people to the gods.

PENDANT A piece of jewellery that hung from a necklace.

PHARAOH The king of Egypt.

PRIESTS People who carry out special duties in a temple or church.

SACRED Special or holy.

SCARAB A beetle which the ancient Egyptians believed was lucky. The scarab was sacred to the Sun God.

SCRIBES People who trained and worked as writers.

SEMI-PRECIOUS STONES Gemstones such as garnet, torquoise, carnelian and lapis lazuli.

SHADUFS Contraptions used to pull water up from the river, to water crops.

TEMPLES Buildings where the gods were worshipped.

TOMB-ROBBERS People who broke into tombs and pyramids and stole the treasure inside.

TOMBS Places where dead bodies were buried.

Index